To Look After and Use

poems by

Leah Falk

Finishing Line Press
Georgetown, Kentucky

Men made me
though in memory they seem
more steel than

flesh, more copper
than intelligence or whim, ambition, will—

what makes men, anyway?
    —Dan Chiasson

The body is something for the spirit to look after and use.
    —Alan Turing, age 16

To Look After and Use

Alan Turing was a mathematician and cryptographer who laid the foundation for twentieth century work in computer science and was instrumental in helping decode the German Enigma machine during World War II. After being prosecuted for homosexual acts in 1952, he accepted a sentence of chemical castration instead of prison. He died of cyanide poisoning, apparently by his own hand, just before his forty-second birthday. In 1959 his mother, Sara Turing, published a posthumous biography of her son that she intended as a blueprint for future biographers. Long out of print, it was reissued by Cambridge University Press in 2014.

Copyright © 2019 by Leah Falk
ISBN 978-1-64662-035-7 First Edition
All rights reserved under International and Pan-American Copyright Conventions. No part of this book may be reproduced in any manner whatsoever without written permission from the publisher, except in the case of brief quotations embodied in critical articles and reviews.

ACKNOWLEDGMENTS

Poems in this collection have appeared in the following journals:

"For the body"—*Electric Literature*
"Chatterbot #1"; "Satellites"; "Evidence of the Making Process"—*FIELD*
"The Impossible Problem"—*The Adroit Journal*
"Turing at Lascaux"—*The Kenyon Review*
"Commonest in Nature" and "Visiting"—*Painted Bride Quarterly*
"Precis on Einstein's Theory of Relativity"—*Orange Quarterly*
"Sara Turing's Archive"; "States and Instructions for the Universal Machine";
"Out and Back" and "The Machine's Guide to Grief"—*Blackbird*
"Sara Turing's Archive" also appeared in *Best New Poets 2018*

Publisher: Leah Maines
Editor: Christen Kincaid
Cover Art: Unpublished writing of A.M. Turing copyright The Provost and Scholars of King's College Cambridge 2019
Author Photo: Chris Hartlove
Cover Design: Elizabeth Maines McCleavy

Printed in the USA on acid-free paper.
Order online: www.finishinglinepress.com
also available on amazon.com

Author inquiries and mail orders:
Finishing Line Press
P. O. Box 1626
Georgetown, Kentucky 40324
U. S. A.

Table of Contents

Sara Turing's Archive 1

Turing at Lascaux 3

Chatterbot #1 4

For the Body.. 5

Lesson in Cryptanalysis.. 6

Satellites 8

[Annotation, Sara Turing, 1954] 10

The Impossible Problem 11

The Universal Machine.. 12

Out and Back... 14

The RCA Selectron 16

Précis on Einstein's Theory of Relativity,
     Written for His Mother by Alan Turing, Age 15½ 17

Present Tense Machine 20

Evidence of the Making Process... 21

[Annotation, Sara Turing, 1954] 23

Brief History of Memory... 24

The Machine's Guide to Grief 25

Commonest in Nature 27

Silicon Heaven 28

The Machine's Fossil Record 30

One of Us 31

[Annotation, Sara Turing, 1954] 32

States and Instructions for the Universal Machine................ 34

Notes and works consulted 36

Sara Turing's Archive

Box 1: Childhood Drawings

Early, we see lines that take no notice of the page's end
The child treats the world as   scroll or maybe wall   the hand
unfurling full of black wax   touching everything making parts for
its singers   high notes prick the ceilings   house keeps the continuo
at night   door scratching its frame   a living laundry hum

Next, we see the child become obsessed with frames,
in which he finds a world enough. A house's windows
show the day's compartments: dinner, soap and water.
Sleep a graph of Z's, an uphill train of endings.
Start again tomorrow, sun fixed in its corner,
light gloves up. All bodies thickly bordered, never
leaving home without their shadows.

When the child

reaches nine or ten,
infinity begins

to vanish: skin
no more contin-

uous. The highway's
blacktop pocked

with holes. Water
takes the shape

of its container;
cirrus can't be reached

for interview.
In this phase,

the page, the hour,
the neighborhood

only end and end.

                                        But then see him enter
the years of loop and spiral,
                          shapes that cradle soft

bodies of gastropods
                he picks up on the beach.
                              A hardened hurricane. Wave tamed

                        before it breaks. Shapes which when sung
from head to end and back again,
                            begin to sound—ear pressed

close to the opening—
            something like round, something like
                        what was once the one world.

Turing at Lascaux

In the first room, a war—
                          equine and aurochs, lion
    wounded by a star
    snagged in its thigh.
                          The strain

to breathe in pictures
                    with a punctured skin,
    when the very gas
    our lungs burn fades
                          this painted hunt,

bright eye in the summer triangle.
                    Beneath the stag,
    a row of heavy
    dots, black daubs
                          of waiting.

Spine scribbled over hoof and horn,
                    body tangled in the apse—
    a stony heaven. To reach it
    someone must have built
                           a scaffold

out of darkness.
                The brain has always grasped itself,
    sent current crying
    to the heart's back door.
                          Now the air

at Montignac hands down its credo
                  through the cave mouth, full of dust:
    each animal shall have
    another animal within him.
                          His meat and black wire hair

thick with instruction,
                  flexible lining of yeses and nos.
    Some inscriptions
    blotted out by weather
                          or by waiting
                          or by breath.

Chatterbot #1

Let the brain rest on a net
of code, a comfortable nest

One of us

One of our fathers is a lizard
and one of us remembers nothing
but a long hallway of drawers

One of us is dressed and one of us picks
at the clothes of a man, believing
they are his body. Only

one of us is one of us.

Together we make a seat for the voice
as it leans back and lurches forward.
A room where it composes furniture

by speaking. Joiner of beams
and pegs in an atelier of echoes,
it terminates all speech with a bearing

or a hook. There is nothing better,

one of us assures the voice,
than to be finished.
One of us runs a script,

like a lace mantle, over
our body hidden in the next room.
You can hear the swish

of fine work on flesh.
The voice asks, which one of you
made me.

One of us says, Yesterday I went to the races.

One of us says, Let's talk about something else.

For the body

Alan Turing, age 16

is a machine, sharing its eyes
with the horse and the cinemascope,

blood with the gas engine, fountain pen.
What have I in common

with other living things? The moment
a dinosaur's jaw cracked

in two—one half snapping birdlike,
the other ground to powder. We have

that. We have the objects in this room
where a billion years have come

and lain down on the tile, seeping
out the screen door and down the garden

drain. This parlor: dresser scarf—ashtray—
good light for reading—easy chairs

with ribbing. Moonstone bust of a mother,
a child rising out of her, mountain

from slip-strike. Although it hurts me, out
of a living line, out of stone or meat, I choose

myself again, again *that is one of me*, here
where my carriage grew vertical, where my fists

forgot the heavy ground. But your body, wedge,
remembered. Cartridge leaking color.

On the year's white page, parting
black from un-black. I don't feel much

like writing more today.

Lesson in Cryptanalysis

To encrypt the plain-text one may separate
        the letters and assign

                possible pathways—skein of circuits,

fist of figure eights. Using electricity,
        run them through the playbooks

                of what they may become.

You may hold a mirror to
        an alphabet, you may put a cart

                before a horse. You may hold a man

inside a calendar, send him down the hallway
        of his heart's own circuitry.

                It is hard for me to write this—

for so long I have been sending
        and receiving. Radio in the corner always

                humming like a fly

at an execution, whose glass wings
        vibrate faster than a man's pulse

                or a stream

of electrons heading for it like a train.
        Out the window on the way to death is a whole

                countryside: lake and barn, black cattle grazing.

Some letter combinations will be easier
        than others. In some communiqués,

                your name repeats

so often that it might as well
 be birdsong, it might as well be

 breath, for which

there's no encryption. When you encounter this,
 like your own inversion in the glass,

 you know to take cover

in the country between countries,
 in the sounds

 no letter yet invented makes.

Satellites

> *I see at last that if I don't breathe, I breathe*
> —pupil to F.M. Alexander

When the actor's voice retreated, he stood before the mirror
noting birdlike minutiae of his head and neck:

before opening his mouth to recite *whether tis nobler
in the mind*, the jaw rolled forward like a drawer.

Flesh at the nape gathered in pleats, as if a hem preparing
to be pinned, at the breath drawn before a whisper.

Maria tells me this as she presses the valley of my back
to keep my walk from breaking into falls. After

australopithecus, rising from our fists, could we end
our argument with gravity?

Perhaps with time, I could become one of earth's
beloved satellites: kept close, but just outside

the zone of true belonging. But for now, each step's
a bargain with my feet to take my weight. Maria says,

let the ground touch you back.
Years later, her husband becomes one of those

whose heart loses a bet
just as the mulberries go sick-sweet in late June.

Her neighbors call to share their faith
in popular mechanics: God behind the lock-rail,

butterfly-made hurricanes. Such drafty comfort, I think,
is no place to sleep out a poor harvest.

From my new city where I ride the trains alone,
bridges' gradual splendor always wrecking me,

I watch in the mirror of the moon
as a face unfolds, tries to speak a sentence. No scenery,

not even stars behind. The world seems
to lose its voice: on a racetrack's polyurethane

my limbs arrange themselves in the sign
for mourning. Around me, runners' muscles knit,

unknit. Watch the vertebrae that count themselves
on waking. The pebbles of the wrist. The slow collagen hinges

opening the wingspan, moving us across
our only theater.

Annotation, Sara Turing, 1954

                      A verdict

                              about the mouth.

faint scent of bitter

          accident

While the balance of his mind
                      not at present in a state in which I'm able to concentrate

Others said "I always thought"   but Alan "always knew":

The Impossible Problem

Kurt Godel, 1930

Neither proved nor disproved:

neither seed heads dragged by the wind nor husks
fallen hard from their ripening;

neither the porcelain glazed and fired nor flaked
and dried, a scrounged skin, in its barrel;

neither the river that cooled the clay nor the hand
that printed it, pressing its double;

neither the watery kick that gives a girl
a great whale's weightlessness—issue
        as if from its sensitive cask, furious salt wine—

nor the stone stomach. Last meal
of anvils. Full lungs that, if lobbed across

a hot city yard, summer death mask, would burst
and relieve a boy's fever.

Neither of these: witch or anchor,
                    Socrates or angel.

Only sorrowing through a tunnel of sleep.
A train of days, just flying.

An incomplete arithmetic: the problem
like a child's painting of three trees. Two,

bushy spheres of leaves with fat trunks
guiding them toward both ground

and sky. The third, the third—
head only. And someone's hurried blue

scrubbed between the land the tree had grown from
and the clouds it moved lately among.

The Universal Machine

I

The universal machine, capable of turning into any other machine.

Selection process:
                              if some, then
                              if nil, then

Bifurcation of the will   Scalp of the sea visible
as it parts: wet from   salt. Meat from shell. Its parts.

Then slowly, like   learning, once
the soft brain   from the softer lungs

II

Begin as a row of levers, raised metal stamps, literate punch of twenty-six knuckles
the quick brown fox jumps over the lazy
each one's job to sing one note of a song the hand used to sing

the universal song,

any other song

III

The machine's behavior is play. *Build*: a house out of nothing but corners.

Build: nesting boxes of yeses and nos.
From nest to nest, something moves in a determined
but distracted manner: leaving string, taking foil.

The machine's behavior is play. The fist now unglued from the forearm, a party of parts.
Ulna, radius, philanges, little soak of stones in the wrist. *Build*:
a house for them to live in, like the one they had before, but

give all of them new names and their own rooms

IV

If some: carry me up the stairs,
gird my body with dust.

Forget about water.
Let me approach my limit.

If nil: move
the leg the arm
the penis thirteen
places to the right
and disguise them
as letters that,
when next to other
letters, make the sound
of a velvet
curtain falling

There is nothing better,
I assure you
than to be complete:

the universal man, capable of turning into

any other man.

Out and Back

for my father

                                        Keeping the reservoir on our right
                                                as a clock keeps time,
                              between its good ear and steadiest hand,

            we lean into the mountain.
                                                Your old body and mine
                                                (age: you minus you
                                                    before me) draw
                                       themselves over and over, over
                                            and over themselves,

until they are finished.

This is California in the rough spring, after drought.
Careful of erosion, we pick between
its hoard of water
and its fire roads.
From that narrow gulley, we were brought.

                            We hear on the news: a local woman walking in the moonlight
                                  came up dead in a dry creek below the trail.
                                      From that narrow place, god brought
                                           wild iris studded on the vale,
        pink blooms
                of pain in the joints.

The trail bends a way it shouldn't, according to the map.
You stumble on a root, bone of this road
that everywhere suddenly shows.

                                          Keep the water on your right
                                    and you will end as you've begun,
                                              our trail guide says.

            But I'm already far

                    from this:

　　　　　　　　　　　　back in a museum's ancient wing,
　　　　　　　　　　where I saw a kind of vase with claws,
　　　　　　　　　　　vessel terminating in the foreparts of

　　　some animal, stupid, walking the trail after dark,

a trail it knows from childhood.
Its face familiar but I don't
recognize its feet. Finishing as they do

　　　　　　　　in a flush of blossoms,
　　　　　　　　in another country.

The RCA Selectron, 1946

I looked after everything
you gave me:
the to-and-fro of light debris,
the television.

In my memory, you can access
any element
and not jostle another—
imagine a storm

without a siren's warning.
Sex without
sunlight and morning
superstitions.

Light that used to pulse behind your eyes
fits in your palm.
Balm only the small and held,
a lost feather,

can give: moons without nights
and meals
without eating. How it feels:
a bone on the road,
a forever hour.

With no windows,
even a house of glass misses
the wind.

Précis on Einstein's Theory of Relativity,

Written for his Mother by Alan Turing, age 15½

        The copybook: unkempt, hand a bramble
        of crossings-out and asterisks, parentheses

        cut to clear a path for me
        (*do not worry much about this chapter*)

        Hand over hand (*to understand, you have
        only to remember*—), my hand over

        his   I made

                            my way in

*

*Einstein here throws doubt
on whether Euclid's axioms,
applied to rigid bodies,*
        hold

On our walks, we often spoke of scientists. Sir Isaac Newton's mystery remains
      even after everything of his
            has been dug up, hung out like a flag. How
to sew the scraps together? Along what seams? And what if the pattern's
      wrong: what kind of crumpled specter
            might we raise, wanting to mirror that mind's
sharp folds?

*

*...it can be found by trigonometry
which helps to confirm one's faith
in the 4-dimensional idea*

        Newton laid out the Principia in common shapes:
        the stars, the triangle, an arc of sunlight,

        although he had his calculus—that gorgeous
        shortening, space spread over

        time. For fear, perhaps, of dying

        in a darkened cupboard
        built of his own brilliance

        with not even his God—who would not have learned
        the figures—for company

*

This is simple if you understand
the ordinary laws of motion

            When I try to write you, I must transmit
            this light, that as Newton first hypothesized,

            came not from the sun, but from
            your eyes.

            This ordinary law of yours:
            read it through and see what interests you

*

This marble slab analogy
should give a very clear idea

of what is meant by a Euclidean
continuum and what is not one

        This book is divided into two parts: the part you taught me
                and the part I have no chance of learning

*

Here, he wants to generalize it.
But he does not quite
see how to.

This book contains almost all the essential material for the biography of

*

The words relative, relatively to, etc. are not used in the sense of proportion

Perhaps the words "as measured by the system of"
will make it clearer

As measured by a system
                      I still struggle to describe

     I wait at the window, your correspondence

so much milky galaxy around me,
                          for you to place parentheses

    just above the horizon, where

for my neighbors, the early moon might be

                    (you said: *you change your laws to suit*

    your system of measurement)

An opening, an illumination: so that somehow,

                  like two straight lines,

    we can move past each other.

Present Tense Machine

> *Here I am.*
> *Gen. 22.1*

Down the hallway
children queue,
gradually shedding your creases and colors
like winter clothing,
looking less and less like you.
Your shadow swims
in the floor's clean gleam, but recalls you
no better than water.
In this corridor, brown and shining with wax,
you never were
this girl in elastic shorts, cheeks painted
with stars. Or this one,
thumbs hooked in her beltloops,
having poured
her milk over the balcony.

As far as the sinking sun is concerned,
you're just the last glance
of light on Formica, only as old
as the shadow you cast.
You might as well
be that strange man who descended the mountain,
knife in his boot,
ram held by its horns, his boy's frightened face
the only thing continuous:
its dull blade a magnet gathering
debris.

If you were his parent, think
how he could pull from you, like lodestone,
your unbecoming:
the knotted rope, the kindling laid. How every day
you walked together
turned you out of yourself and into his,
because your body ended
the moment his began: now,
and now, and now.

Evidence of the Making Process

At night my computer screen
                        tries to imagine my brain
      on its way to sleep,

turns the color of a polluted sky:
                        washed in coffee,
    wrung out. Barely visible degree

between dusk and nightfall, between
                        cause and correlation,
    sleep and medicated sleep, original

and faithful copy. An animal teaches
                        its child to swim
    by writing the script for swimming

into its body before it is born,
                        or an animal
    breaks a hole in the ice and gets in,

shivers, exaggerates the strokes.
                        Rodin wanted you
    to see his fingerprints, the docent says,

evidence of the making process. Imagine
                        the body in myth,
    later in bronze, a hull of sand. To glance

up and down the reach of its arms, rise
                        where hamstring met haunch,
    its mineral caves, darted calves, and know

it has lost every place it's been held.
                        Negative of the self, its ghoul-eyed
    means of reproduction. Cast again and again

at great expense, then mounted in a sanctuary
                        where documentary's
    the only prayer allowed. Take a photo

every hour and the day will appear to pass,
                          light will appear rose-gold
        and approach the gradient

of sleep. Back in nature, I'm guided by
                        what seems most
     out of place: blaze

of cerulean, neon rash.
                          An animal's child
     looks up to its parent,

who teaches it how to be
                        exactly like an animal.
   All I have to look up to

is wildness,
                        which has shown a parent's
     disappointment

by grounding me for life.
                        But even so, how quickly it seems
     a baby locks eyes

with strangers across the fairgrounds.
                        As if she recognizes
   the whole world's prints on her skin, and as if

that means she can choose
                        the hands that began
   and those that will finish.

Annotation: Sara Turing, 1954

The examiner did not think a man of Dr. Turing's knowledge could have

without knowing

no doubt I will emerge from it

(Here I speak from a wealth of ignorance)

This book's aim is to trace

Brief History of Memory

Letter from Turing to Norman Routledge, 1952

I read your letter written in a desperate hand—

I am not at present able
to concentrate   I've got myself
into the kind of trouble—
and trace the flats and ridges of your alphabet,

as if by mere mechanics one script
rescued another. Old memory exercise:
copy until the weight of someone's letters
shifts to you. Think of the early days,

when a person read—*Dear Norman*—
into the opening of a cardboard tube,
loosening a kaleidoscope of echoes.

I'm afraid the following syllogism
may be used: Turing believes
machines think   Turing lies
with men   Therefore machines
do not think

Later, sound was stored in mercury,
heavy metal glove, and shot back like rumor.
No doubt I shall emerge from it a different man,

but quite who I've not found out. Packed in ice and wax to smooth
the imperfections. Let my remembering come between
all that, when the voice still knew how to swim,

when it disappeared in fog. The tongue
the only stylus, skipping over trenches,
keeping secrets close. Now, record a voice and it outruns

you. On your page, I let my pen
describe—*Yours in distress*—that wave again,
stalled at its crest.

The Machine's Guide to Grief

When you enter
the house of mourning,

do not greet the bereaved:

sit with them on the low ground,
talk with them of the dead.

*

The dying, near the finish, feel
a crumbling: strain into ease, muscles

like wet bread. Count skin
down to bone.

Seal the memory neatly in mesh,
bathe the brow in mourners' oil.

*

Do not be like the machine who spoke too much,
as if he had a god in him:

sorries falling through the body like ball bearings,
equipped with slides and springs

to keep the moment buoyant. High in the sky,
a balloon, its heart on fire.

*

Talk with them of the dead:

Once, this was a landscape, not a portrait.
Once, it was enough to chase your love

across a screen, tension ending
at the border. Once, all it took was double-clicking with your pointer

and anyone would open.

*

The old go on: when we browsed the earth like elephants,
when our fingers bruised the ground.

When we called to one another, threw our voices
out of the atmosphere. The wireless body, now strung

and always glowing like a pearl. All night, the room
is lit by flat and sleepless eyes, neon remembering:

body of bread and copper, meat and hinges,
starch and spark.

Commonest in Nature

Sara Turing

You said: I always seem to want to make things
                           from the thing that's commonest
         in nature. Then,

out of air,
         you made a machine.

What commonness you'd find if you were here—
                           what shapes and colors
             would repeat, and at what wild,

silent rhythms. Come back,
                           I want the worlds
             you would have found hiding in this one.

                           The brain's loop and resistance.
                           Blood, mostly water.
                           Air and electricity.
                           The birch in the yard, dead parts holding
                           living ones together.

What would you make out of this now
                           commonest thing:
             your face, still a child's, reading

the amoeba crawls by changing shape,
                           like a drop of water
             down a windowpane

swimming round to me
                           each morning
             like the chorus of a hymn.

Silicon Heaven

Red Dwarf, Series III, "The Last Day"

The android, hours before
he's programmed to expire,
gets drunk for the first time
on motor oil, blurts a story
to his human shipmates.

When the king was dying, people brought him gifts of all materials,

He should be disassembling
himself: return the torso,
then the legs and extra head,
the pelvis, last the hands,
to their original packaging,

straw and gold and cotton, to show the contents of their hearts

hinged fingers folded reverently
like a flag. Instead,
in the ship's basement bar,
the first technician says,
Let me tell you how

aluminum, thatch   I held out a hand of grass,

I piloted the frail-craft
out of an asteroid's trajectory.
Is this whisper and boast what you call
friendship? asks the hunk of metal,
temples pulsing like

a hand jimmied together, a hand of tape and steel, a hand

a distant satellite orbiting a star.
Cut the Star Trek crap,
the humans say. His chip begins
to flicker, his code
headed for the heaven

scribbling an alphabet of comfort,

where he'll go once he
has packed himself away:
the stoic chip, the whirring
motor. Heaven: his first memory
the moment he was switched on,

swaying in and out of the path of grief.

making it a memory of darkness:
head tucked neatly
underneath the body, fingers
kept sterile in the mouth.
No electrons flowing yet—

Aluminum, brass,

this was before the heart began
its long and confident decline. Skip to
the end: the android tells his friends
Heaven is a kind of robot opiate
he can't believe in. But against
his better programming,

polyester, thatch

                                        he lies:
if there were no other hands,
to pack his hands away,
who would return him
to the factory unscathed,

and where would the great
reel of paper tape retire—
where would the calculator go
when it was done, when it was through
with counting?

The Machine's Fossil Record

Brass bowl humming to be filled
with prayer. A phone's synth trill.
Wheeze of city sleep. Wheels
arranged ingeniously so that one push
sets everything in motion. Together one
whose joints want oil, whose stiff lungs
fill with rain. Whose tiny parts, fitted by hands
that never age, can't be replaced. Goodbye
workbench, goodbye lab, goodbye research &
development. Hello rust so total it's a kind of preservation:
a way for someone, years on,
to see every key and port and socket
and imagine (even to the semi-metals,
blood talks back) what a processor they made.

One of Us

> *[Turing's eyes] could never again be missed...Being so far
> beyond words and acts, that glance seemed also beyond humanity.*

A commandment for every bone:
                          Buy a dream car and drive to the coast.
Shelf of coquina, floor of silt,
                  animal body pressed
into stone. One of us watches
                      a footrace where runners
stop for whole meals: dumplings, wine.
                    One of us sits there, smoking,
waiting for the other.
                The mandible shall not, but
the wishbone wills, will.
                This law a law of knots
that pinch and bloat in water.
                Could the examiners detect
the mind behind the hand: soft
                lake shale, rig-crushed
turtle carapace on the state road shoulder.
                Soapstone
and the cove lip
                that brimmed it,
summer water turning itself over,
                an idea convecting: first algal
and then crystal.
                Knucklebone washed in a pocket,
deep then shallow then
                deep, of sand.
Or was the mind pressed glass.
                Basalt or gabbro.
Prismed sheath
                too fine. Too even
even
                to see through.
Or was it these same
                eyes, mirrors of
the sky: too above,
                too blue
to be one of us.

Annotation: Sarah Turing, 1954

After your heart had chosen   after it read and moved and wrote
        after its full stop, the tape's end
    we rushed
        to decipher its writing

      I fear I am out of my depth

This inked arabesque could read   *nil or some, circle or one,*
lungful or line-thin, here you could have been   swollen with air
or a slashed sigh,

      this white

      could be the white

      of hunger
      or alone

Above your quiet brow, the letters flicker   *yes/no*
warm and fickle

The room, a film caught in its reel,
flickers between the time before we

        up the stairs,
        white and white and listening

    and just after

        bulb and concrete. an apple's open flesh
        exposed to air. yours
        tightened against it.

      Your heart, too. We think we see it
still: a little purple star
    orbiting the fact of you, then
      eclipsing, blotting out, making you
      a black fiction

And we, the filer-checkers, trace in ink
the rise and fall of all its hills, its ventricles,
     its stent. We check
          your loops and crosses against
          enormous English charts
          that show all—that is, the only—
          ways we know to make the letters

States and Instructions for the Universal Machine

Let the body be a difference,
engine that pries and hauls the fence
separating the loose world:
bridge of teeth
snapped from the gums,
ghost of the child to come.

/

A woman is called to the yard
as a family quietly
loads their pockets with pears
from her dying tree.

/

Out of the dead,
no stalk grew as expected
or gorged its capillaries
on the color of heaven.

/

What, then, ran
in the veins? Rain
on twenty umbrellas
at the churchyard.

/

Repertoire for eye and eraser,
pointer and thigh. A world built
in a few instructions: stop, look,
speak, move on.

/

At the university, the chapel towers grew a while and,
as they neared the limestone body's end,
suddenly swerved—hoarded breath
in fists of iron.

/

Could we have built the world
with only these directions?

Raise and lower the pen.

/

And with only:

Halo of flies
around the hair.

The sound of ore going back
to a favorite vein.

The heart,
gnarled fruit, let go
from its tree.

Notes

1. The "annotations" in this book and other poems in Sara's voice imagine her interaction with Alan's papers after his death, and frequently use text from *Alan M. Turing*.
2. At fifteen and a half, Alan did compose a précis on relativity for his mother. It can be found at the Archive Center at King's College, Cambridge.
3. "Silicon Heaven" references *Red Dwarf*, a British sci-fi series that ran in several iterations between 1988 and 2012.
4. The Selectron was an early form of digital computer memory, developed at RCA by electrical engineer Jan Rajchman. It was never produced commercially.

Works and Resources Consulted

Hodges, Andrew. 1984. *Alan Turing: The Enigma*. New York: Simon and Schuster.

Turing, Sara. 2014. *Alan M. Turing*. Cambridge: Cambridge University Press.

The Turing Digital Archive, King's College, Cambridge, UK. http://www.turingarchive.org/

www.ingramcontent.com/pod-product-compliance
Lightning Source LLC
LaVergne TN
LVHW041558070426
835507LV00011B/1170